How Women's Participation in Conflict Prevention and Resolution Advances U.S. Interests

COUNCIL *on*
FOREIGN
RELATIONS

DISCUSSION PAPER

How Women's Participation in Conflict Prevention and Resolution Advances U.S. Interests

Jamille Bigio
Rachel Vogelstein

October 2016

This Discussion Paper was published under the auspices of the Women and Foreign Policy program in conjunction with the Center for Preventive Action.

The Council on Foreign Relations (CFR) is an independent, nonpartisan membership organization, think tank, and publisher dedicated to being a resource for its members, government officials, business executives, journalists, educators and students, civic and religious leaders, and other interested citizens in order to help them better understand the world and the foreign policy choices facing the United States and other countries. Founded in 1921, CFR carries out its mission by maintaining a diverse membership, with special programs to promote interest and develop expertise in the next generation of foreign policy leaders; convening meetings at its headquarters in New York and in Washington, DC, and other cities where senior government officials, members of Congress, global leaders, and prominent thinkers come together with CFR members to discuss and debate major international issues; supporting a Studies Program that fosters independent research, enabling CFR scholars to produce articles, reports, and books and hold roundtables that analyze foreign policy issues and make concrete policy recommendations; publishing *Foreign Affairs*, the preeminent journal on international affairs and U.S. foreign policy; sponsoring Independent Task Forces that produce reports with both findings and policy prescriptions on the most important foreign policy topics; and providing up-to-date information and analysis about world events and American foreign policy on its website, CFR.org.

The Council on Foreign Relations takes no institutional positions on policy issues and has no affiliation with the U.S. government. All views expressed in its publications and on its website are the sole responsibility of the author or authors.

For further information about CFR or this paper, please write to the Council on Foreign Relations, 58 East 68th Street, New York, NY 10065, or call Communications at 212.434.9888. Visit CFR's website, www.cfr.org.

Contents

Acknowledgments

This report is the product of several consultations with CFR's advisory committee on women, peace, and security, a distinguished group of experts in the national security, foreign policy, and human rights communities. Over the past several months, members of this advisory committee have participated in meetings, reviewed drafts, and shared research and insights from their work. The report has been enhanced considerably by the expertise of this advisory group. The views expressed herein and any errors are our own.

A special acknowledgment is extended to James M. Lindsay, CFR's director of studies, for his support for this project and Paul Stares, senior fellow for conflict prevention and director of the Center for Preventive Action, for his partnership in this effort. We are grateful to Patricia Dorff and Sumit Poudyal for their review of previous drafts and to Anne Connell, Becky Allen, Alexandra Eterno, and Lucy Leban for their excellent assistance in the production of this paper. U.S. officials also provided feedback that significantly contributed to the report.

This report was made possible in part by the generous support of the Compton Foundation and the CFR Women and Foreign Policy Advisory Council.

Jamille Bigio
Rachel Vogelstein

Introduction

Recurrent and emerging armed conflicts, expanded terrorist and extremist networks, increased targeting of civilians, and record levels of mass displacement have defined global security in the twenty-first century. Data shows that standard peacemaking methods have proved ineffective at addressing these trends: nearly half of the conflict resolution agreements forged during the 1990s failed within five years.[1] Recidivism for civil war is alarmingly high, with 90 percent of civil wars in the 2000s occurring in countries that had already experienced civil war during the previous thirty years.[2] New thinking on peace and security is needed.[3]

A growing body of research suggests that standard peace and security processes routinely overlook a critical strategy that could reduce conflict and advance stability: the inclusion of women. Evidence indicates that women's participation in conflict prevention and resolution advances security interests. One study found that substantial inclusion of women and civil society groups in a peace negotiation makes the resulting agreement 64 percent less likely to fail and, according to another study, 35 percent more likely to last at least fifteen years.[4] Several analyses suggest also that higher levels of gender equality are associated with a lower propensity for conflict, both between and within states.[5]

Despite growing international recognition of women's role in security, the representation of women in peace and security processes has lagged. Between 1992 and 2011, women represented less than 4 percent of signatories to peace agreements and 9 percent of negotiators (see figure 1).[6] In 2015, only 3 percent of UN military peacekeepers and 10 percent of UN police personnel were women, substantially lower than the UN target of 20 percent.[7] And despite the role that local women's groups could play in preventing and resolving conflicts, they received just 0.4 percent of the aid to fragile states from major donor countries in 2012–2013.[8]

Given the rising number of security threats and growing evidence that women's participation in peace and security processes improves stability, women's inclusion merits a higher place on the U.S. foreign policy agenda. While the U.S. government has advanced a comprehensive policy framework to promote the role of women in security under successive Republican and Democratic administrations, more action is needed to realize its promise. The next U.S. administration should require women's representation and meaningful participation in conflict resolution and postconflict processes, increase investment in efforts that promote women's inclusion, reform U.S. diplomatic and security practices to incorporate the experiences of women in conflict-affected countries, improve staffing and coordination to deliver on government commitments, strengthen training on incorporating women in security efforts, and promote accountability. These steps will help the United States respond effectively to security threats around the world, improve the sustainability of peace agreements, and advance U.S. interests.

The Case for Women's Participation in Security

Despite the historical exclusion of women from negotiating tables and security apparatuses, the evidence of women's contributions to conflict prevention and resolution is growing. Several empirical analyses confirm that women offer unique, substantive, and measurable contributions to securing and keeping peace. Evidence shows that security efforts are more successful and sustainable when women contribute to prevention and early warning, peacemaking, peacekeeping, and post-conflict resolution and rebuilding. A qualitative evaluation of women's influence in recent peace processes—notably in Guatemala (1996), Northern Ireland (1998), Liberia (2003), and the Philippines (2014)—further illustrates the critical role that women can play in resolving conflict and promoting stability.

PREVENTION AND EARLY WARNING

Research suggests that women can improve the efficacy of conflict prevention and early warning strategies. Women's central roles in many families and communities afford them a unique vantage point to recognize unusual patterns of behavior and signs of impending conflict, such as arms mobilization and weapons caching. In Kosovo, for example, women were the first in their communities to voice concerns when young men were amassing weapons, heading into the local hills, and training. Although Kosovar women reported signs of impending conflict well before violence broke out, no adequate reporting systems were in place to capture and make use of their insights.[9]

Evidence also indicates that incorporating women in strategies to counter violent extremism can help to mitigate radicalization. Although traditional efforts by governments and nongovernmental organizations to combat radicalization typically focus on reaching out to political or religious leaders—who are predominantly male—recent research shows that antiterrorism messages are effectively disseminated throughout families and communities by women, who are well placed to challenge extremist narratives in homes, schools, and social environments, and have particular influence among youth populations.[10] In recognition of the critical role that women can play in countering terrorism in families and communities, several governing bodies have taken steps to integrate women into their antiterrorism strategies. The Organization for Security and Cooperation in Europe, for instance, has invested in the Sisters Against Violent Extremism global initiative, one of the first women-centered anti-extremism platforms and training programs.[11] The 2016 joint U.S. State Department-U.S. Agency for International Development (USAID) strategy to counter violent extremism around the world explicitly recognized that women's groups can help to identify and address the drivers of violent extremism within their families, communities, and societies.[12] The United Kingdom (UK) applied this approach domestically in its 2011 national counterterrorism policy, in which it committed to partner with women to amplify prevention measures at the community and family levels.[13]

In many countries, women are well positioned to detect early signs of radicalization because their rights and physical integrity are often the first targets of fundamentalists.[14] A qualitative analysis of interviews with nearly three hundred people in thirty countries across the Middle East, North Africa, and South Asia found that women were substantially more likely than men to be early victims of extremism.[15] Indeed, restrictions on women's rights have accompanied the rise of extremist groups—particularly those with fundamentalist religious ideologies—across the globe, as has been documented with the Taliban in Afghanistan, the self-proclaimed Islamic State group, and Boko Haram in Nigeria.

In addition, research shows that women's participation in early warning mechanisms can help mitigate instability during election cycles that are frequently marred by violence triggered by perceptions of flawed electoral processes or political and ethnic tensions. For example, Women's Situation Rooms (WSRs)—innovative, real-time groups convened around election cycles to anticipate and combat electoral violence—have been employed to provide a mechanism through which women in populations at risk of conflict contribute to prevention efforts by documenting grievances, resolving community-level disputes, and reporting electoral offenses, thereby providing critical intelligence to national or regional early warning systems for electoral violence.[16] WSRs have been implemented successfully in Kenya, Liberia, Nigeria, and Senegal. Ahead of Kenya's 2013 general election, for instance, women leaders from Liberia, Nigeria, Tanzania, and Uganda assisted Kenyan leaders in establishing a WSR. Trained election observers, dispatched across the country, addressed over five hundred registered complaints—including threats to candidates and voters—and relayed information to the electoral commission and the police. Women's involvement helped to de-escalate tensions that many had feared would fuel a replication of the violence that had followed Kenya's 2007 election, which resulted in 1,300 deaths and thousands displaced from their homes.[17]

PEACEMAKING

Women's participation in formal peace processes also contributes to the achievement and longevity of peace agreements. A qualitative review of forty peace and constitution-drafting negotiations since 1990 found that parties were significantly more likely to agree to talks and subsequently reach an agreement when women's groups exercised strong influence on the negotiation process, as compared to when they had little or no influence.[18] Another study, which analyzed 181 peace agreements signed since 1989, found that when women had participated in peace processes as witnesses, signatories, mediators, and/or negotiators, the resulting agreement was 35 percent more likely to last at least fifteen years.[19] Additional research examined all peace agreements in the post–Cold War period and found that participation of civil society groups, including women's organizations, made a peace agreement 64 percent less likely to fail.[20]

Analysis of prior peace processes suggests that women's participation increases the likelihood of an agreement because women often take a collaborative approach to peacemaking and organize across cultural and sectarian divides.[21] Research suggests that such an approach—which incorporates the concerns of diverse demographics (e.g., religious, ethnic, and cultural groups) affected by a conflict and with an interest in its resolution—increases the prospects of long-term stability and reduces the likelihood of state failure, conflict onset, and poverty.[22] Numerous case studies have documented instances where women built coalitions across ethnic, political, religious, and sectarian divides, including in Afghanistan, Colombia, Guatemala, Iraq, Northern Ireland, Somalia, and South Africa.[23] In Afghanistan, for example, women, who made up only 20 percent of the delegates to the 2004 constitutional convention, successfully reached across ethnic lines to push for a commitment to equal rights for all Afghan citizens and to support efforts by the Uzbek minority to gain official recognition for its language.[24] Even in cases where women have limited or no access to formal governmental talks—known as track one negotiations—and instead are limited to track two nongovernmental talks, as in Guatemala (see Country Profiles), women's groups often use backroom roles to facilitate input to formal, track one negotiators and provide insight from marginalized groups that may otherwise not be heard.[25]

Including women at the peace table can also increase the likelihood of reaching an agreement because women are often viewed as honest brokers by negotiating parties. This perception is rooted in the reality of women's exclusion: because women often operate outside existing power structures and generally do not control fighting forces, they are more widely perceived to be politically impartial mediators in peace negotiations, compared with men.[26] The proposition that women are seen as trustworthy negotiators is empirically supported. For example, in-depth interviews with negotiators from the Burundi, Northern Ireland, and South Africa peace processes found that the ability of female representatives to build trust, communicate, involve all sides, and settle disputes encouraged parties to negotiate and compromise.[27] Recent history suggests that women are rightfully considered to be reliable peace brokers: a review of forty peace processes since 1990 found that no women's group sought to derail a peace process.[28]

Women often advance peacemaking by employing visible and high-profile tactics to pressure parties to begin or recommit to peace negotiations, as well as to sign accords. Women's groups have successfully staged mass actions and mobilized public opinion campaigns in many countries to encourage progress in peace talks, with notable examples in Burundi, Colombia, Democratic Republic of Congo (DRC), Liberia (see Country Profiles), and Somalia. In DRC, for instance, forty female delegates to the 2002 Sun City talks formed a human chain to block the exits from the committee room, insisting that delegates remain until the signing of a peace agreement.[29] In Somalia, women observers at the 1993 Conference of National Reconciliation staged a public fast until an agreement was reached—a pressure tactic that produced a peace plan twenty-four hours later.[30] Moreover, where peace deals are put to public referendum, women's groups have frequently launched national campaigns to persuade voters to approve the negotiated agreement. For example, the Northern Ireland Women's Coalition was at the forefront of a civil society campaign that strengthened public support for the 1998 referendum of the Good Friday Peace Agreement (see Country Profiles). In recent times, women's groups have organized more mass action campaigns in support of peace deals than any other social group.[31]

Ensuring diversity at the negotiating table has also been shown to contribute a breadth of perspectives that can advance conflict resolution. Because women tend to have different social roles and responsibilities than men do, they have access to information and community networks that can inform negotiating positions and areas of agreement. In 2006, for example, when negotiations in Darfur deadlocked over control of a particular river, local women advised the male negotiators—who were rebel group leaders living in the diaspora—that the river in question had dried up several years prior.[32] Women had access to critical knowledge—in that case, borne of their disproportionate responsibility to fetch water—that helped to break an impasse.

Women's inclusion in peace talks not only advances the likelihood of achieving a resolution but also contributes to the sustainability of an agreement, partly because women are more likely to raise social issues in negotiations that help societies reconcile and recover. Evidence suggests that women frequently raise issues in conflict resolution processes beyond military action, power-sharing arrangements, and territorial gains, instead introducing political and legal reforms, social and economic recovery priorities, and transitional justice concerns that can make agreements more durable.[33] The International Crisis Group's research in DRC, Sudan, and Uganda indicates that during peace talks, women often raise issues of human rights, security, justice, employment, education, and health care that are fundamental to conflict resolution and postconflict rebuilding.[34] In the Northern Ireland peace negotiations, for example, women pushed to include provisions on social and economic priorities, such as integrated housing and education; in Darfur, women delegates recommended the inclusion of provisions on food security, protection for internally displaced persons and refugees, and the prevention of gender-based violence, all of which advance long-term stability.[35] Women's inclusion in conflict resolution processes also increases the chance that peace agreements will address the particular needs of vulnerable groups in postconflict situations, thus promoting reconciliation; for example, women are more likely to advocate for accountability and services for survivors of conflict-related sexual violence.[36]

Despite the evidence of women's critical contributions to peace processes, in the last twenty-five years, women represented only 4 percent of signatories to peace agreements and 9 percent of negotiators (see figure 1).[37] Signatories to peace agreements are typically heads of state or party, or represent the top echelons of armed groups, and are, therefore, disproportionately male. Continued failure to include women and civil society actors in peace processes ignores their demonstrated effectiveness and overlooks a critical strategy to advance peace and stability.

The vast majority of peace agreements reached in the last three decades failed to refer to women or their conflict experiences, including conflict-related sexual violence (see figure 2).[38] This trend has slightly improved since the adoption of UN Security Council Resolution 1325 in 2000, which committed to support women's participation in peace negotiations. Between 1990 and 2000, 11 percent of peace agreements referenced women; the proportion rose to 27 percent for agreements signed between 2000 and 2014.[39] However, only a handful of those agreements include more than one provision addressing the concerns and priorities of women, and few of these have been implemented.

FIGURE 1. WOMEN'S ROLES IN MAJOR PEACE PROCESSES, 1992–2011

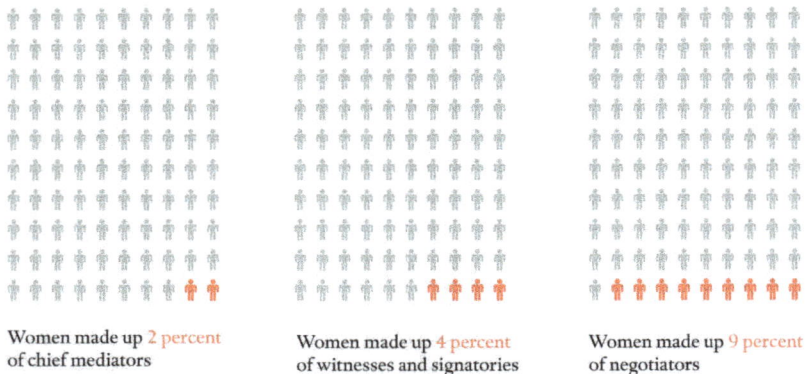

Women made up 2 percent of chief mediators

Women made up 4 percent of witnesses and signatories

Women made up 9 percent of negotiators

Source: Pablo Castillo Diaz and Simon Tordjman with Samina Anwar et al., "Women's Participation in Peace Negotiations: Connections Between Presence and Influence," UN Women, October 2012.

FIGURE 2. REFERENCES TO WOMEN AND GENDER-BASED
VIOLENCE IN PEACE AGREEMENTS

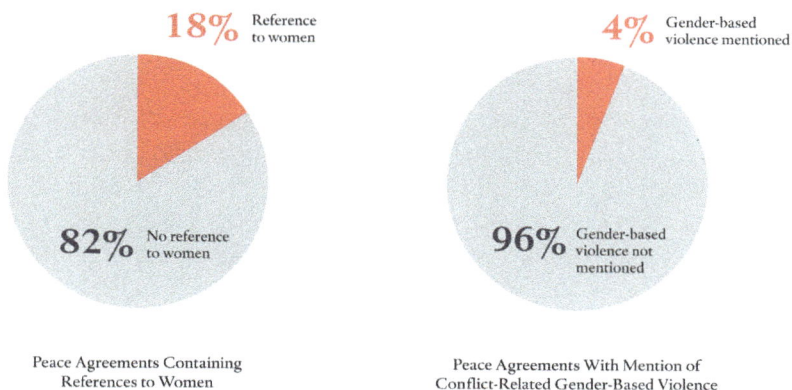

18% Reference to women

82% No reference to women

Peace Agreements Containing
References to Women

4% Gender-based violence mentioned

96% Gender-based violence not mentioned

Peace Agreements With Mention of
Conflict-Related Gender-Based Violence

Analysis of 1,168 peace agreements 1990–2014

Source: Christine Bell, "Text and Context: Evaluating Peace Agreements for Their 'Gender Perspective,'"
University of Edinburgh, Global Justice Academy, UN Women, March 2015.

PEACEKEEPING

Evidence suggests that women make unique and substantive contributions that improve the effectiveness of peacekeeping operations. UN assessments have found that women peacekeepers are fully able to perform the same roles to the same standards as their male counterparts, even in hardship posts. When women do participate, research shows that they gain access to information that male counterparts often cannot obtain: particularly in traditional cultures, female security sector officials frequently have access to populations and venues that are closed to men, which allows them to gather intelligence about potential security risks.[40] Female officers are also better able to respond to concerns about women's physical safety. Data from thirty-nine countries demonstrates that women are more likely to report instances of gender-based violence to female officers—a finding anecdotally supported for police, military, and peacekeeping personnel.[41]

Women's participation in the security sector also measurably improves dispute resolution. Research indicates that women in police forces are less likely than male counterparts to use excessive force and are more likely to de-escalate tensions.[42] Female security sector officials also help institutions build trust with the communities they serve, thereby advancing stability and the rule of law: women's participation in the security sector is associated with fewer misconduct complaints and improved citizen perceptions of force integrity.[43]

A visible presence of female peacekeepers has been shown to empower women and girls in host communities and can raise women's participation rates in local police and military forces.[44] In Liberia, observers attributed an increase in women's participation in the national security sector—from 6 percent to 17 percent in nine years—to the example set by the UN peacekeeping mission's all-female police unit deployed there in 2007.[45]

Despite evidence that women's inclusion in peacekeeping and security sector roles offers considerable benefits, women are routinely underrepresented. In 1993, women made up just 1 percent of the United Nations' deployed uniformed personnel, and in 2015, only 4 percent of military peacekeepers and 10 percent of police personnel were women—far short of the UN target of 20 percent.[46]

POSTCONFLICT RECOVERY AND REBUILDING

Recent analysis also suggests that ensuring diversity—including through women's participation—in postconflict recovery and rebuilding processes advances stability. One study found that commissions charged with delivering on specific aspects of a peace agreement—such as monitoring disarmament, establishing a truth and reconciliation process, or drafting a constitution—were more effective when women participated.[47] Women's inclusion in disarmament, demobilization, and reintegration (DDR) efforts after the Liberian conflict offers a concrete example: when initial DDR activities led by the UN Mission in Liberia (UNMIL) resulted in unrest, women's groups went to the cantonments to ease tensions, open dialogue with former combatants, and protect children, ultimately providing recommendations that strengthened UNMIL's future efforts.[48] In Sierra Leone, 55 percent of ex-combatants interviewed in one study identified women in the community as central figures in aiding reintegration, compared with 32 percent citing international aid workers and 20 percent citing community leaders.[49]

Evidence also indicates that women are more likely to direct postconflict resources to the reconstruction of public institutions and provision of services critical to stability. High levels of women's participation in public sector positions—as police officers, judges, agricultural extension agents, teachers, or medical attendants—can improve the quality of service delivery for entire communities. One study in India found that women-led villages invested more in drinking water and infrastructure; immunized more children; and had lower gender gaps in school attendance, lower levels of corruption, and greater levels of women's political participation as compared with communities led by men.[50] Another study, in Kenya, found that women's participation in water and infrastructure committees significantly improved community access to water: female representation in these communities resulted in a 44 percent decrease in the likelihood that access to drinking water would require more than a sixty-minute walk.[51]

Research supports the notion that strengthening women's political and social participation after conflict diminishes the chance of conflict relapse. An analysis of fifty-eight postconflict states between 1980 and 2003 found that the risk of conflict relapse was near zero when women made up at least 35 percent of the legislature; when women were unrepresented in parliaments, however, the risk of relapse increased over time.[52] Higher levels of women's political participation are also associated with a lower risk of civil war onset and a reduced likelihood of state-perpetrated political violence—fewer killings, forced disappearances, instances of torture, and political imprisonments.[53] Furthermore, countries are more prosperous and stable as the gender gap closes across a range of areas, including access to education and health care, political participation, and economic participation: in one cross-cutting study of conflict-affected communities, the most rapid postconflict reduction in poverty was observed in areas where women reported higher levels of empowerment.[54] Failure to invest in women in postconflict situations, therefore, undermines the potential for prosperity and stability.

POTENTIAL CRITIQUES

Skeptical foreign policy and national security experts caution that involving new actors—including women's groups—in a negotiation could threaten already fragile deliberations.[55] Evidence shows otherwise: women's participation as negotiators, experts, or representatives of civil society in fact decreases the threat of spoilers to negotiations, increases public perception of legitimacy, and improves the likelihood of reaching and sustaining a peace agreement.[56] While designing and structuring any peace process presents significant challenges, setting preconditions—including with respect to the composition of negotiating delegations and the scope of talks—is common practice. Adding a requirement for women's representation fits within this preexisting set of considerations.

Traditional culture is also cited as a threat to the feasibility of women's participation in peace and security processes. The concern that promoting women's participation might be culturally inappropriate overlooks the fact that, from Afghanistan to Yemen, local actors in conservative societies have led calls for gender quotas and for other decision-making processes to include women's perspectives. Furthermore, women's participation in a peace or transition process can present an opportunity to lay the groundwork for a more equitable and prosperous future for a postconflict nation, given strong evidence that advances in women's participation across economic, political, and social lives are correlated with prosperity and growth.[57]

Others claim that women's inclusion in peace and security processes is not possible because of a dearth of women with the necessary technical expertise. Indeed, in most regions of the world, women have limited experience in national politics and the armed forces because they are dramatically underrepresented. However, this gap is closing due to training and capacity-building; in many cases, local civil society organizations and international mediators have identified a pool of highly qualified female negotiators and experts to offer to delegations prior to negotiations. Despite these efforts to train and identify women to participate in peace and security processes, studies find that women in peace processes face greater scrutiny of their credibility and qualifications than their male counterparts do, and parties to armed conflict consistently fail to work with women's groups or seek qualified women.[58]

Some scholars and policymakers dispute the notion that women's participation in peace and security processes will garner better results, arguing that women are not universally peaceful. Indeed, leaders from Golda Meir to Margaret Thatcher have taken their countries to war, and women around the world serve in combat roles and encourage their husbands, brothers, and sons to participate in conflict. Recent analysis shows that extremist organizations, including the Islamic State, recruit women for logistical activities, operational leadership, and suicide bombing.[59] In fact, these examples demonstrate that women are influential in whatever capacity they serve—whether as moderating and peaceful forces in a community or as armed combatants or military leaders—and, therefore, it is critical to involve them in both the prevention and resolution of conflict.

Critics also maintain that there is not enough evidence establishing women's contributions to peace and security efforts to justify spending critical resources or time promoting their integration. Indeed, given the historical exclusion of women from security apparatuses and peace processes, there are fewer examples of women's positive influence in this arena than in others. However, as detailed above, empirical analyses strongly suggest that women's participation in early warning and prevention, peace-building, peacekeeping, and postconflict recovery processes is associated with improved outcomes. Qualitative analyses of country case studies further demonstrate how women's meaningful participation can strengthen peace or transition processes. While the evidence of the effect of women's participation in peace and security processes will grow as women's representation increases, even current knowledge suggests that overlooking the contributions of 50 percent of the world's population is a strategic handicap.

COUNTRY PROFILES

A qualitative evaluation of women's influence in peace processes of the past twenty years—notably in Guatemala (1996), Northern Ireland (1998), Liberia (2003), and the Philippines (2014)—further demonstrates the critical role that women can play in resolving conflict and promoting stability. Women in Guatemala raised critical priorities through a formal civil society forum, and women in Northern Ireland furthered peace talks by establishing a new political party. In Liberia, women lobbied negotiators to resolve an impasse by waging a grassroots mass action campaign, and in the Philippines, women helped to lead negotiating teams to an interim resolution of the conflict. In each case, women shaped the negotiation agenda and strengthened the content of a peace agreement.

GUATEMALA

Guatemala's 1996 peace accords concluded a bloody thirty-six-year civil war. The negotiated cease-fire reached between government forces and leftist insurgent groups ended a conflict that inflicted on civilians atrocities such as sexual violence, torture, campaigns of terror, and forced disappearances. In the decade-long process that led to the 1996 ceasefire, civil society organizations—including women's groups—were active in the Civil Society Assembly (ASC), a forum through which they identified issues that otherwise would not have been heard. Public participation in the process resulted in the inclusion of nearly two hundred distinct and substantive commitments on social, economic, and political reforms in the final accords.[60]

Many of these reforms were introduced and championed by women in the ASC's women's sector with members from different sections of Guatemala's population that had been affected by the conflict, including ethnic Mayan and rural communities, students, human rights activists, and trade unions.[61] This group promoted a broad agenda that included land tenure reform, social justice, and the establishment of the Office for the Defense of Indigenous Women—proposals that addressed the core grievances of rural Guatemalans that had ignited the conflict, thereby increasing the likelihood of a sustainable agreement.

Within their communities, women promoted stability by organizing campaigns for disarmament and successfully pressuring neighbors to give up their weapons, as well as developing strategies to help former fighters move into productive work.[62]

NORTHERN IRELAND

Following the Troubles, which had left over 3,600 dead and thousands more injured, the 1997 peace talks offered Northern Ireland a chance to resolve the intractable conflict between Irish Catholic nationalists and British Protestant unionists. The 1996 electoral system had allotted two seats to negotiators from any valid political party—an unusual design that provided women's groups an opportunity to gain formal access to the talks.[63]

Monica McWilliams, an Irish Catholic, and May Blood, a British Protestant, successfully gathered signatures to incorporate as a political party so that they could participate in the formal peace process. Their Northern Ireland Women's Coalition (NIWC) garnered support from women across religious lines, drew on a strong network of grassroots women's peace organizations, and brought a unique perspective to the negotiations. Helen Jackson, a member of the British Parliament and an observer at the negotiations, later noted that this group "gave a human face to the conflict, and highlighted the personal consequences of war." NIWC developed a reputation as an honest broker that could facilitate dialogue between parties and secured language in the Good Friday Agreement that specifically referenced victims' rights and provided for reintegration of political prisoners, education, and mixed housing.[64] These were issues that the main parties to the conflict had never before brought forward but that ultimately proved to be fundamental to promoting social cohesion after the conflict and to sustaining peace.[65]

LIBERIA

After the 1989 coup, in which Charles Taylor assumed the presidency, Liberia spiraled into two successive waves of armed violence, the second of which killed over two hundred thousand people and displaced one-third of the country's population. Although the combatants were mostly men, women and girls across the country were subjected to widespread sexual violence, abductions, forced labor, and forced marriages.

In April 2003, a group of Liberian women led by activist and future Nobel Peace Laureate Leymah Gbowee launched Women of Liberia Mass Action for Peace. The national nonviolent campaign brought together Muslim and Christian women from different ethnic and class backgrounds to demand an end to war.[66] Gbowee reflected that "in the past we were silent, but after being killed, raped, dehumanized, and infected with diseases . . . war has taught us that the future lies in saying no to violence and yes to peace."[67]

The group became instrumental in forcing formal talks, holding belligerents accountable to negotiation timetables, and mobilizing national support for the process. The group met Taylor and successfully pressured him to participate in peace talks in Accra, Ghana. In Accra, women staged a sit-in and refused to let any party leave the premises before they reached a negotiated resolution; the talks culminated in the signing of the 2003 Comprehensive Peace Agreement.

After the cessation of hostilities, women led a nationwide voter and civic education campaign that reinvigorated public trust and participation in the political process. Subsequent elections brought into power the country's first female head of state, Ellen Johnson Sirleaf, and resulted in higher female representation in the security sector. In recognition of women's contributions to peacekeeping, the Liberian

National Police ultimately adopted an ambitious 20 percent quota for women in the police and armed forces, and established recruiting and training programs to expand the pool of women qualified for service.[68]

THE PHILIPPINES

For forty years, armed conflict simmered between the government of the Philippines and various Moro rebel factions that sought to establish an independent Muslim-majority Mindanao Island, resulting in over 6,000 deaths between 1989 and 2012.

Women played active roles in both formal and informal negotiations in the Mindanao peace process that ended open hostilities in 2014. Miriam Coronel-Ferrer, who led the Philippine government's team in peace negotiations with the Moro Islamic Liberation Front, was the first woman chief negotiator in history to sign a major peace accord. Women held meaningful positions on the negotiating teams of both parties to the conflict, in part because of the Philippine government's support for international frameworks for women's rights, including UN Security Council Resolution 1325.[69]

Throughout the peace process, women fostered a feedback loop between diverse groups and different negotiation tracks. Civil society organizations, including women's groups, provided recommendations to the track one process, drawing on information gathered in their parallel nongovernmental talks. Women's groups also were active in grassroots campaigns to gather input for the formal peace process and relay updates to the public, leading extensive national consultations with a cross section of religious and indigenous people, youth, and other groups.[70] A subsequent evaluation found that Moro women were better able than men to preserve interethnic alliances as tensions in the Filipino-Mindanao conflict escalated; this ability fostered channels of communication and provided information about threats of violence that could derail the peace process.[71]

The resulting agreement recognized women's contributions to transitional governance: for example, the agreement guaranteed women's inclusion in new institutional bodies and promoted women's economic participation as a critical pillar of a broader national strategy for growth.

Policy Considerations for the United States

CURRENT U.S. POLICY

In recent years, as the evidence of women's contributions to peacemaking and peacekeeping has grown, women's role in conflict resolution and security has received greater international attention. In 2000, the United Nations adopted Security Council Resolution 1325 under the leadership of Namibia and with strong support from Bangladesh and other Security Council members. This was the first of eight resolutions to date through which the United Nations formally recognized the importance of women's participation in conflict resolution and postconflict reconciliation processes and committed to promoting their involvement. As of 2016, over sixty countries—from developing nations like Afghanistan and Kenya to high-income countries like Japan and the UK—have developed National Action Plans on Women, Peace, and Security, a tool recommended by the UN Security Council to enable countries to advance national efforts to increase women's participation in security processes and improve women's protection from threats of violence (see figure 3). Regional and multilateral bodies from the African Union to the North Atlantic Treaty Organization (NATO) to the Group of Seven (G7) also have outlined commitments to support women's participation in preventing and resolving conflict.

Notably, the U.S. government has taken significant steps to advance the role of women in peace and security processes. At the United Nations, the United States led the adoption of critical Security Council resolutions aimed at combating sexual violence in conflict. During the George W. Bush administration, the U.S. government championed Security Council Resolution 1820, which declared that rape and other forms of sexual violence in conflict can constitute war crimes, crimes against humanity, or acts of genocide. Under Barack Obama, the United States led efforts to enact Security Council Resolution 1888, which established

FIGURE 3. COUNTRIES WITH NATIONAL ACTION PLANS ON UN SECURITY COUNCIL RESOLUTION 1325

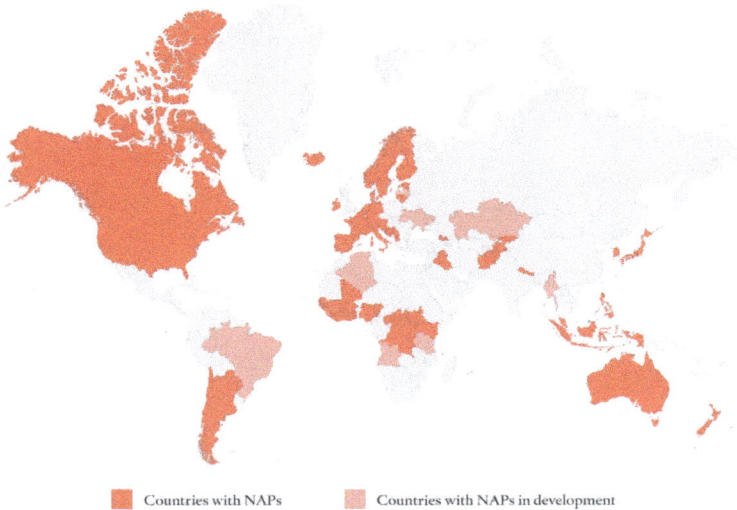

Countries with NAPs   Countries with NAPs in development

Source: Women's International League for Peace and Freedom, "National Action Plans for the Implementation of UNSCR 1325 on Women, Peace, and Security," May 2016, http://www.peacewomen.org/member-states.

a special representative to the UN secretary-general on sexual violence in armed conflict to promote greater attention to this issue.

These efforts laid the groundwork for a new U.S. policy framework on women and security, starting with the 2010 U.S. National Security Strategy, which recognized that countries are more peaceful and prosperous when women are accorded equal rights. In 2011, the U.S. government expanded on this strategic commitment by enacting a National Action Plan. The U.S. plan included commitments by the Departments of Defense, State, Justice, Treasury, and Homeland Security; the U.S. Mission to the United Nations; USAID; the Centers for Disease Control and Prevention; and the Office of the U.S. Trade Representative. Its issuance was accompanied by an executive order directing its implementation and requiring an evaluation of progress, which culminated in an updated plan, released in 2016. The plan pledged to institutionalize a gender-sensitive approach to diplomatic, development, and defense-related work in conflict-affected areas, including by increasing women's participation in conflict prevention and postconflict processes;

strengthening efforts to prevent and protect women from violence; promoting women's roles in conflict prevention, both through early warning and response systems and by elevating the status of women generally; and ensuring women's access to humanitarian assistance. Other new policies enacted by the Obama administration—including global plans to combat gender-based violence and trafficking in persons, as well as internal guidance requiring national security and foreign assistance agencies to elevate a focus on gender equality—complement the work prescribed under the National Action Plan.[72]

However, the development of a strong policy framework on women, peace, and security at both the international and national levels has not significantly improved women's participation in conflict prevention and resolution. By 2015, which marked the fifteenth anniversary of UN Security Council Resolution 1325, only one woman—Coronel-Ferrer—had ever served as a chief negotiator for a peace agreement, and only one woman—Mary Robinson—had ever served as a UN chief mediator. International peace negotiations continue to proceed without the consistent inclusion of women in positions of influence, including in Afghanistan, Iraq, and Syria. Despite the strong evidence-backed case for women's participation in peace processes, decision-makers—including government officials, conflict or negotiation parties, mediators, and other international actors—often consider women's inclusion to be a normative duty rather than a strategic need that would benefit the process and improve the sustainability of peace agreements.[73] While many U.S. security policies today note the importance of women's participation—from atrocity prevention to the prevention of violent extremism and security sector assistance—this imperative has not been prioritized or allocated resources at levels that would improve women's participation or strengthen outcomes.

In the U.S. Congress, bipartisan groups in the House and Senate have reintroduced legislation to bolster implementation of the U.S. National Action Plan, including in the areas of conflict prevention, humanitarian and disaster response, conflict mediation, peacekeeping, postconflict reconstruction, institution-building, and democracy promotion. Although earlier components of the draft bills were included in broader legislative proposals, to date, efforts to codify and resource the U.S. National Action Plan have languished.

In recent years, the United States has taken steps to incorporate women into its national security apparatus. Although a 1994 rule prohibited women from serving in combat roles, since 2001, more than 300,000 women have been deployed to Afghanistan and Iraq to serve in noncombat positions; some women were deployed directly into combat as participants in cultural support teams.[74] Following extensive review of the effect of women's combat participation on unit cohesion, women's health, equipment requirements, and other issues, the United States officially opened all combat roles to women in 2015. Women currently make up around 15 percent of the active duty force of the U.S. Department of Defense (DOD), and while they are 20 percent of the officer corps, they hold less than 10 percent of leadership positions.[75] Women are represented at higher levels in U.S. diplomacy and development agencies: at the State Department, they represent 45 percent of entering Foreign Service officers and 31 percent of senior Foreign Service officers; at USAID, they hold close to half of all mid- and senior-level management positions.[76]

RECOMMENDATIONS FOR THE UNITED STATES

The next president will inherit significant security threats at home and abroad, at a time of restricted budgets and economic uncertainty. In light of these challenges, some critics will suggest that expending money and time to advance women's roles in peace and security processes would be an unnecessary distraction. Notwithstanding these constraints, given the significant evidence that women's participation in peace and security processes will strengthen U.S. conflict prevention and resolution efforts, the next administration should advance the role of women in security. Investing time and resources to increase women's participation where it is lacking will improve the likelihood that peace and security efforts are successful and sustainable, thereby saving lives and resources in conflict-affected countries as well as in the donor countries—including the United States—that send troops or invest otherwise in resolving the conflict.

Despite the claims of critics that it is culturally inappropriate for the United States to encourage women's participation in conservative societies around the world, there are qualified female leaders in conflict-affected countries—from Afghanistan and Yemen to Colombia and South Sudan—who can and want to contribute to peace and security.

Providing them the opportunity to do so requires modest financial and technical support. Failure to support them would ignore the growing body of research confirming that the inclusion of women is a critical strategy to reduce conflict and increase stability.

As one of the largest financial supporters of peace and security efforts around the world, the United States can not only make its own operations more effective by investing in inclusive conflict prevention and resolution but also set an example for others to follow, thereby strengthening security efforts around the world. U.S. diplomacy could be better deployed to encourage conflict-affected countries to include women in peace and security efforts, while U.S. resources to promote women's training and participation could inspire similar investments from other donor countries. The United States is thus uniquely positioned to improve security by catalyzing international efforts to empower women in countries affected by conflict, violence, and instability.

However, a significant gap remains in translating rhetoric to action. Notwithstanding the enactment of a U.S. National Action Plan on women, peace, and security, support for women's participation in security processes is not yet standard practice across U.S. agencies, and there are many missed opportunities where women's contributions could have improved the effectiveness of U.S. operations. Shifting this trend requires a new level of commitment by the United States and holds the potential to significantly improve stability efforts around the world.

To strengthen U.S. conflict prevention and resolution efforts, the White House—together with the Departments of Defense, State, Justice, and Treasury and USAID, among other agencies—should accelerate implementation of the U.S. National Action Plan and better integrate women into peace and security processes.

REQUIRE REPRESENTATION

Given clear evidence of women's contributions to peace and security efforts, the United States should promote women's participation in peace and security processes by establishing as precondition to its involvement in a peace or transition process that negotiating bodies and mediating teams include a significant representation of women in formal roles—with a target of at least 30 percent, a threshold that research suggests affords a critical mass to enable women's influence.[77] Furthermore, negotiators and mediators should consult civil society—including women's groups—on the design, implementation, and monitoring of any peace agreement, and should ensure the protection of women leaders at risk of targeted political violence, including assassination.[78] These steps will help guarantee that women have the opportunity to inform and influence the design, implementation, and evaluation of peace agreements and peace-building mechanisms, thereby improving the likelihood of reaching and sustaining peace agreements.

Given that women are consistently underrepresented in international delegations to peace and security processes, such as observer missions and mediation support teams, the U.S. government should also ensure that its delegations consist of at least 30 percent women—and encourage the European Union, United Nations, and other international actors to do the same. Any instance of less than 30 percent representation by women should prompt an internal review.

To increase representation of women at all levels of government in postconflict countries, U.S. support for public institutions—including the armed forces, police services, and the judiciary—should include technical assistance to promote the recruitment, retention, and advancement of women. Effective measures to promote women's participation in government include quotas, fast-track promotion plans, legal prohibitions on discrimination against women, and technical training, complemented by efforts to facilitate networking and professional development.

INCREASE INVESTMENT

Despite significant U.S. investment in conflict prevention, countering violent extremism, and other defense priorities, few resources are allocated to promoting women's participation in security efforts—an omission that overlooks the benefits of women's participation and the contributions of half the population. To maximize the return on defense investments, the U.S. government should increase resources to facilitate women's involvement in peace and security processes by adopting the United Nations' funding target to provide a minimum of 15 percent of all peace-building and security assistance for conflict-affected countries to promote women's participation and protection.[79] The 15 percent funding target also should apply to rapid response funds, such as the Complex Crises Fund, managed by the State Department and USAID.

FIGURE 4. FY 2017 U.S. FOREIGN OPERATIONS BUDGET REQUESTS TO ADVANCE GENDER EQUALITY

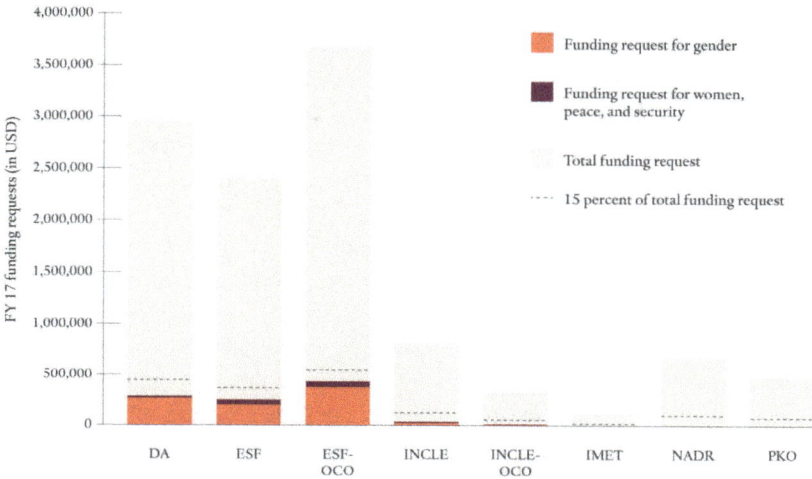

Development Assistance (DA); Economic Support Fund (ESF); Economic Support Fund-Overseas Contingency Operations (ESF-OCO); International Narcotics Control and Law Enforcement (INCLE); International Narcotics Control and Law Enforcement-Overseas Contingency Operations (INCLE-OCO); International Military Education and Training (IMET); Nonproliferation, Antiterrorism, Demining and Related Programs (NADR); Peacekeeping Operations (PKO)

Source: "Congressional Budget Justification, Department of State, Foreign Operations, and Related Programs; Fiscal Year 2017," U.S. Department of State, February 9, 2016, http://www.state.gov/documents/organization/252179.pdf.

To reach the 15 percent target, the DOD, State Department, and USAID should include funding to advance women's participation in security processes at the outset of the budget process (see figure 4). Peace and security-related programs should support efforts to advance women's participation as primary or cross-cutting funding goals—rather than secondary or incidental effects—and explicitly identify gender requirements in program budgets and results frameworks. The State Department and USAID also should collaborate with partner governments, as well as multilateral entities like the G7, to fund long-term support for local women's groups to promote women's leadership in security processes. At least 10 percent of any grant to a local women's group should support technical capacity-building to promote the efficacy and inclusion of local women's groups in conflict resolution and postconflict processes.

REFORM DIPLOMATIC AND SECURITY PROCESSES

The United States should better articulate how incorporating women's participation in peace and security processes advances its strategic interests in prosperity and stability around the world. Within the first one hundred days of the next U.S. administration, the president should issue a statement supporting the role of women in conflict prevention and resolution, and identify ten to twenty time-bound, measurable goals—either global or country-specific—that are fully funded and assigned to particular government agencies. This step will make concrete the broad commitments of the 2016 revised U.S. National Action Plan and help the administration track and deliver on its commitments.

Senior U.S. officials assigned to fragile states or regions—including ambassadors, USAID mission directors, and combatant commanders—should be required to approach local women leaders and women's organizations within the first thirty days of their arrival, followed by semiannual meetings. U.S. officials also should include issues raised by women's groups in high-level bilateral processes, including strategic dialogues, in order to advance effective policy options.

Internal security procedures—from conflict assessment to program design and reporting and evaluation mechanisms—should incorporate the experiences and perspectives of local women and girls. Similarly, early warning systems should draw on women's networks to better anticipate and respond to potential threats and opportunities, including those related to conflict, atrocities, and electoral violence. All community-level efforts to prevent and counter terrorism and violent extremism should involve women leaders and women's groups, given their potential to prevent or mitigate radicalization of family and community members.

Doctrine and strategic plans—from integrated country strategies to country development coordination strategies and theater campaign plans—should indicate how women's involvement contributes to specific security-related priorities. To expand on the authority and specificity of the current DOD guide for implementing the U.S. National Action Plan, a formal DOD instruction should provide services and combatant commands with more detail on specific activities they can undertake to promote women's contributions to security, including by assigning responsibility to particular offices and instituting reporting requirements. Where national governments have established priorities to advance women's participation in security processes—such as through the development of a national action plan—the U.S. government should support their efforts through funding and technical assistance.

IMPROVE STAFFING AND COORDINATION

The U.S. government should ensure that senior U.S. officials have access to the tools and assistance needed to deliver on the government's commitments. In addition to financial resources, the U.S. government should provide human resources, including at least one full-time senior-ranking coordinating position at the DOD, State Department, and USAID. For any peace-building program above $10 million, implementing partners should have at least one part-time gender advisor.

In Washington, the National Security Council staff should host monthly meetings that identify priorities in support of women's contributions to security and coordinate with existing regional and security structures, such as the Atrocity Prevention Board. In all fragile states, U.S. government officials should participate in any donors' gender working group, identify common objectives, and co-invest where possible; where gender working groups do not exist, the U.S. government should use its convening power to work with local partners to establish them. Additionally, in all fragile states, the U.S. government should establish internal gender working groups—composed of representatives from across the embassy, including political sections, USAID security and governance experts, and defense attachés—that report to the ambassadors. Similarly, each of the armed service branches and combatant commands should host working groups focused on gender considerations in military operations. These working groups have proved to be instrumental in facilitating intra-government collaboration and increasing the likelihood of policy and program success. Where a security situation is of strategic importance to the United States, the U.S. ambassador-at-large for global women's issues, together with USAID and DOD counterparts, should host a monthly dialogue with the U.S. embassy's internal gender working group to improve coordination and increase the effectiveness of U.S. efforts.

STRENGTHEN TRAINING

U.S. government staff—including foreign and civil services—and contractors working in security-related fields or focused on fragile states should participate in at least one training related to women's participation in peace and security processes. Such training should detail how the inclusion of women increases the effectiveness of security-related policies and programs, and outline steps that staff can take to promote women's participation. Curricula should include scenario-based training that prepares personnel to involve women in prevention and peacebuilding efforts, and the U.S. government should encourage other governments as well as peacekeeping training centers around the world to similarly offer such training.

The U.S. government should offer annual training on women's involvement in peace processes at educational institutions like the U.S. Foreign Service Institute, National Defense University, and DOD regional centers. The joint professional military education should include the topic of women and security in its annual academic priorities to encourage professional military education institutions, such as the Naval War College and the Air War College, to train students on why and how to incorporate women into security efforts.

The U.S. government also should ensure that women in partner countries benefit from training programs for militaries, police forces, governments, and civil society groups. U.S. officials should institute a minimum requirement of 30 percent female participation in all U.S.-offered training related to peace and security issues, from partner military training to elections training in postconflict societies and professional exchanges through international visitor programs.

PROMOTE ACCOUNTABILITY

The United States should report annually on its expenditures on women, peace, and security, including in defense and foreign assistance spending related to building partner military capacity, counterterrorism, conflict mitigation and stabilization, citizen security and law enforcement, and humanitarian assistance. To promote better outcomes, U.S. agencies should rigorously evaluate the effect of their investments on women's participation rates and broader security conditions. The DOD, State Department, and USAID should each fund at least one operational research per fiscal year focused on a specific priority related to women, peace, and security, such as those identified in the new administration's agenda for the first one hundred days. The U.S. government also should commission case studies from recent peace and security processes in which the United States was involved to understand how women advance security interests, and should support additional research on the relationship among gender equality, women's participation, and state stability.

In addition, to promote oversight of the implementation of U.S. commitments to advance women's participation in security, Congress should pass legislation to build on the U.S. National Action Plan and require periodical reporting on progress, such as the S.224 bill on women, peace, and security, and to require steps to increase women's participation in security, including the S.3377 bill to enhance military and police operations through women's engagement and recruitment. The U.S. government should monitor progress on commitments made by multilateral institutions by, for example, using its roles in the UN Security Council, the Peacebuilding Commission Organizational Committee, and the executive boards of UN agencies to assess progress on the implementation of the United Nations' seven-point action plan and its strategic results framework.[80] The United States should also participate in the Security Council's informal expert group on women, peace, and security to consistently draw the council's attention to women's participation in security issues.

Summary of Policy Recommendations for the United States

The next U.S. administration should

- within the first one hundred days issue a presidential statement in support of the role of women in conflict prevention and resolution, and identify ten time-bound, measurable goals;

- set as a precondition of its participation in a peace process that negotiating bodies and mediating teams include a significant representation of women in formal roles—with a target of at least 30 percent—and work with civil society in the design, implementation, and monitoring of the agreement;

- ensure that women represent at least 30 percent of U.S. delegations to peace and security processes, and encourage the United Nations, European Union, and other international actors to do the same;

- provide technical assistance to all public institutions supported by the U.S. government to promote the institutions' recruitment and retention of women;

- adopt the UN target of providing 15 percent of all peace-building and security assistance for conflict-affected countries to efforts that promote women's participation and protection;

- fund long-term support for local women's groups, with at least 10 percent of any grant focused on technical capacity;

- require senior U.S. officials assigned to fragile states or regions to approach local women leaders and women's organizations within the first thirty days of their arrival, followed by semiannual meetings;

- dedicate at least one full-time senior-ranking coordinating position at the DOD, State Department, and USAID; for any peace-building program above $10 million, implementing partners should have at least one part-time gender advisor;

- require all U.S. government staff working in security-related fields or focused on fragile states to participate in at least one training session related to women's participation in peace and security processes;

- require 30 percent female participation in all U.S.-offered training to international partners that relates to peace and security issues;

- ensure that all peacekeeping training centers around the world include scenario-based training to involve women in prevention and peace-building efforts;

- report annually on U.S. government expenditures on women, peace, and security, including in defense and foreign assistance spending;

- fund at least one DOD, State Department, and USAID study per fiscal year focused on administration priorities for women, peace, and security; and

- encourage Congress to pass legislation that would build on the U.S. National Action Plan and require regular reporting on its implementation.

Conclusion

In the twenty-first century, unleashing the potential of 50 percent of the world's population is not just the right thing to do—it is a strategic imperative. Substantial evidence confirms that women's participation in peace and security processes increases the likelihood and sustainability of peace. Nevertheless, women's representation in conflict prevention and resolution efforts has grown only minimally in the sixteen years since the adoption of UN Security Council Resolution 1325, which formally acknowledged the benefits of women's participation. The United States is uniquely positioned to lead by example and catalyze international efforts to improve this record. To respond effectively to modern security threats and address the failure of traditional peacemaking methods, the next U.S. administration should promote women's roles in conflict resolution and postconflict processes, and ensure that the rising generation of American diplomats and security professionals recognizes that women's participation in security efforts around the world advances U.S. stability.

Endnotes

1. "Trends in Human Insecurity," in *Human Security Report 2009/2010: The Causes of Peace and the Shrinking Costs of War*, Human Security Report Project, December 2, 2010, http://hsrgroup.org/docs/Publications/HSR20092010/20092010HumanSec urityReport-Part3-TrendsInHumanInsecurity.pdf.

2. "WDR 2011: Facts & Figures," World Bank, 2011, http://web.worldbank.org/archive/ website01306/web/pdf/english_wdr2011_facts_figures%20no%20embargo.pdf.

3. Marie O'Reilly, "Inclusive Security and Peaceful Societies: Exploring the Evidence," *PRISM* 6, no. 1, March 1, 2016, pp. 21–33; Radhika Coomaraswamy et al., "Preventing Conflict, Transforming Justice, Securing the Peace: A Global Study on the Implementation of United Nations Security Council Resolution 1325," UN Women, 2015, http://wps.unwomen.org/~/media/files/un%20women/wps/highlights/unw-global-study-1325-2015.pdf.

4. Desirée Nilsson, "Anchoring the Peace: Civil Society Actors in Peace Accords and Durable Peace," *International Interactions* 38, no. 2, April 2012, p. 258; Laurel Stone, "Quantitative Analysis of Women's Participation in Peace Processes," in Annex II in Marie O'Reilly et al., "Reimagining Peacemaking: Women's Roles in Peace Processes," International Peace Institute, p. 34; O'Reilly et al., "Reimagining Peacemaking," pp. 12–13.

5. Valerie M. Hudson et al., "The Heart of the Matter: The Security of Women and the Security of States," *International Security* 33, no. 3, 2008/2009, pp. 7–45; Mary Caprioli, "Primed for Violence: The Role of Gender Inequality in Predicting Internal Conflict," *International Studies Quarterly* 49, no. 2, 2005, pp. 161–178; Erik Melander, "Gender Equality and Intrastate Armed Conflict," *International Studies Quarterly* 49, no. 4, 2005, pp. 695–714; Valerie M. Hudson et al., *Sex and World Peace* (New York: Columbia University Press, 2010); James D. Fearon, "Governance and Civil War Onset," Stanford University, August 2010.

6. Pablo Castillo Diaz and Simon Tordjman with Samina Anwar et al., "Women's Participation in Peace Negotiations: Connections Between Presence and Influence," UN Women, August 2010.

7. "Report of the Secretary-General on Women, Peace and Security," UN Security Council, September 2015; "Report of the Secretary-General on Women and Peace and Security," UN Security Council, September 2014, p. 27; "Women in Peacekeeping," United Nations Peacekeeping, http://un.org/en/peacekeeping/issues/women/womeninpk.shtml.

8. "Financing UN Security Council Resolution 1325: Aid in Support of Gender Equality and Women's Rights in Fragile Contexts," OECD DAC Network on Gender Equality, March 2015, http://oecd.org/dac/gender-development/Financing%20UN%20Security%20Council%20resolution%201325%20FINAL.pdf.

9. Felicity Hill, "Women's Contribution to Conflict Prevention, Early Warning and Disarmament," United Nations Institute for Disarmament Research, 2003.

10. United States Institute for Peace, "Charting a New Course," 2015, http://usip.org/sites/default/files/Women_Preventing-Violent-Extremism-Charting-New-Course%20(2).pdf; "A Man's World? Exploring the Roles of Women in Counter Terrorism and Violent Extremism," eds. Naureen Chowdhury Fink, Sara Zeiger, and Rafia Bhulai, Hedayah, Global Center on Cooperative Security, 2016.

11. "SAVE: Sisters Against Violent Extremism," Women Without Borders, http://women-without-borders.org/save; Naureen Chowdhury Fink and Rafia Barakat, "Strengthening Community Resilience Against Violence and Extremism: The Roles of Women in South Asia," Center on Global Counterterrorism Cooperation, November 2013, http://www.globalcenter.org/wp-content/uploads/2013/12/13Nov27_Women-and-CVE-in-South-Asia_Policy-Brief_Final.pdf.

12. "Department of State & USAID Joint Strategy on Countering Violent Extremism," U.S. Department of State and USAID, May 2016, http://www.state.gov/documents/organization/257913.pdf.

13. Women and Preventing Violent Extremism: The U.S. and U.K. Experiences," CHR&GJ, http://chrgj.org/wp-content/uploads/2012/10/Women-and-Violent-Extremism-The-US-and-UK-Experiences.pdf; "The United Kingdom's Strategy for Countering Terrorism," Government of the United Kingdom, July 2011, http://gov.uk/government/uploads/system/uploads/attachment_data/file/97994/contest-summary.pdf.

14. UN Women, "Women and Violent Radicalization in Jordan," 2016, http://www2.un-women.org/~/media/headquarters/attachments/sections/library/publications/2016/women-violent-radicalization-jordan-en.pdf?v=1&d=20160726T143843.

15. Karima Bennoune, *Your Fatwa Does Not Apply Here: Untold Stories from the Fight Against Muslim Fundamentalism* (New York: W. W. Norton & Company, 2013); Karima Bennounce, "Bennoune: Support Muslims Resisting Fundamentalism," speech delivered at the International Peace Institute, October 2, 2013, http://ipinst.org/2013/10/bennoune-support-muslims-resisting-fundamentalism; O'Reilly, "Inclusive Security and Peaceful Societies."

16. "Women's Situation Room," UN Women West and Central Africa, http://unwomen-westandcentralafrica.com/womens-situation-room.html.

17. Coomaraswamy et al., p. 203; Udo Jude Ilo, "Making Elections Count: A Guide to Setting Up a Civil Society Election Situation Room," Open Society Initiative for West Africa, April 2012; "Women's Situation Room: A Unique Type of Response Mechanism in Elections," UN Kenya Newsletter, March 2013, http://unicnairobi.org/newsletter/UNNewsletter_March2013.pdf; "Kenya: Too Early to Turn the Page on IDPs, More Work Is Needed," Internal Displacement Monitoring Center, June 3, 2014, http://internal-displacement.org/sub-saharan-africa/kenya/2014/kenya-too-early-to-turn-the-page-on-idps-more-work-is-needed-.

18. Thania Paffenholz et al., "Making Women Count—Not Just Counting Women: Assessing Women's Inclusion and Influence on Peace Negotiations," UN Women, April 2016, http://inclusivepeace.org/sites/default/files/IPTI-UN-Women-Report-Making-Women-Count-60-Pages.pdf.

19. Stone, "Quantitative Analysis," in Annex II in O'Reilly et al., "Reimagining Peacemaking," p. 34.

20. O'Reilly et al., "Reimagining Peacemaking;" Nilsson, "Anchoring the Peace," pp. 243–266; Thania Pfaffenholz, Darren Kew, and Anthony Wanis-St. John, "Civil Society and Peace Negotiations: Why, Whether and How They Could Be Involved" (background paper, Oslo Forum, 2006), http://american.edu/sis/faculty/upload/Wanis-Civil-Society-and-Peace-Negotiations.pdf.

21. Seth G. Jones and Martin C. Libicki, "How Terrorist Groups End: Implications for Countering al Qa'ida," RAND Corporation, 2008, p. 1; Bennoune, *Your Fatwa Does*

Not Apply Here; "Bennoune: Support Muslims Resisting Fundamentalism;" Chowdhury Fink and Barakat; "Women and Countering Violent Extremism: Summary Document and Analysis," Permanent Mission of the United Arab Emirates to the United Nations and Georgetown University Institute for Women, Peace, and Security.

22. See, for example, Frances Stewart, *Horizontal Inequalities as a Cause of Conflict: Understanding Group Violence in Multiethnic Societies* (New York: Palgrave Macmillan, 2008); Daron Acemoglu and James Robinson, *Why Nations Fail: The Origins of Power, Prosperity and Poverty* (New York: Crown Publishers, 2012); O'Reilly, "Inclusive Security and Peaceful Societies."

23. Patty Chang et al., "Women Leading Peace," Georgetown University Institute for Women, Peace and Security, 2015.

24. Klara Banaszak et al., "Securing the Peace: Guiding the International Community Towards Women's Effective Participation Throughout Peace Processes," UN Women, 2005; Masuda Sultan et al., "From Rhetoric to Reality: Afghan Women on the Agenda for Peace," Hunt Alternatives Fund, February 2005, p. 23.

25. Chang et al.

26. Marie O'Reilly, "Why Women? Inclusive Security and Peaceful Stories," *Inclusive Security*, October 2015, http://inclusivesecurity.org/wp-content/uploads/2015/10/Why-Women-Brief-10.12.15.pdf.

27. Sanam Naraghi Anderlini, "Women at the Peace Table: Making a Difference," UN Women, 2000.

28. O'Reilly et al., "Reimagining Peacemaking," p. 11; O'Reilly, "Inclusive Security and Peaceful Societies."

29. Jane Freedman, *Gender, Violence and Politics in the Democratic Republic of Congo* (United Kingdom: Routledge, 2015), p. 95.

30. Paffenholz et al., "Making Women Count."

31. Ibid.

32. Mobina Jaffer, "Mobina Jaffer (Canada)—Women and Peace Negotiations in Darfur," Institute for Inclusive Security, November 17, 2010, http://youtube.com/watch?v=755YwYpzEmU.

33. See, for example, Sanam Naraghi Anderlini, *Women Building Peace: What They Do, Why It Matters* (Colorado: Lynne Rienner Publishers, 2007); "Inclusive Security, Sustainable Peace: A Toolkit for Advocacy and Action," International Alert and Women Waging Peace, November 2004; O'Reilly, "Inclusive Security and Peaceful Societies;" International Crisis Group, "Beyond Victimhood: Women's Peacebuilding in Sudan, Congo and Uganda," Africa Report No. 112, June 28, 2006; Pablo Castillo Diaz and Simon Tordjman with Samina Anwar et al., "Women's Participation in Peace Negotiations: Connections Between Presence and Influence," UN Women, October 2012.

34. "Beyond Victimhood."

35. Avila Kilmurray and Monica McWilliams, "Struggling for Peace: How Women in Northern Ireland Challenged the Status Quo," *Solutions* 2, no. 2, March 2011; O'Reilly, "Inclusive Security and Peaceful Societies;" Jaffer, "Women and Peace Negotiations in Darfur."

36. Paffenholz et al. 2006.

37. Castillo Diaz et al., "Women's Participation in Peace Negotiations," 2012.

38. Christine Bell, "Text and Context: Evaluating Peace Agreements for Their 'Gender Perspective,'" University of Edinburgh, Global Justice Academy, UN Women, March 2015.

39. Ibid.; "Taking Stock, Looking Forward: Implementation of UN Security Council Resolution 1325 (2000) on Women, Peace and Security in the Conflict Prevention and Resolution Work of the UN Department of Political Affairs (2010–2014)," United Nations Department of Political Affairs, March 2015.

40. Louise Olsson and Johan Tejpar, "Operational Effectiveness and UN Resolution 1325 - Practices and Lessons From Afghanistan," May 2009, pg. 117; pp. 126–127; Institute for Inclusive Security, "Attention to Gender Increases Security in Operations: Examples From the North Atlantic Treaty Organization (NATO)," April 2012, pp. 7–13.

41. Amalia R. Miller and Carmit Segal, "Do Female Officers Improve Law Enforcement Quality? Effects on Crime Reporting and Domestic Violence Escalation," UBS International Center of Economics in Society at the University of Zurich, August 2014, p. 4; UN Women, "Progress of the World's Women: In Pursuit of Justice," Progress of the World's Women series, United Nations Entity for Gender Equality and the Empowerment of Women, 2011, pp. 59–61.

42. Kim Lonsway et al., "Men, Women, and Police Excessive Force: A Tale of Two Genders; A Content Analysis of Civil Liability Cases, Sustained Allegations, and Citizen Complaints," National Center for Women and Policing, April 2002; Katherine Spillar, "How More Female Police Officers Would Help Stop Police Brutality," *Washington Post*, July 2, 2015, http://washingtonpost.com/ posteverything/wp/2015/07/02/how-more-female-police-officers-would-help-stop-police-brutality/?utm_term=.174e7c1ffaac.

43. Kim Lonsway et al.; "Policy Briefing Paper: Gender Sensitive Police Reform in Post Conflict Societies," United Nations Development Fund for Women and United Nations Development Program, October 2007, http://unwomen.org/~/media/Headquarters/ Media/Publications/UNIFEM/GenderSensitivePoliceReformPolicyBrief2007eng. pdf; Tara Denham, "Police Reform and Gender," Geneva Center for the Democratic Control of Armed Forces (DCAF), 2008, p. 5.

44. "Women in Peacekeeping."

45. Lesley J. Pruitt, "The Women in Blue Helmets," University of California Press, June 2016.

46. "Report of the Secretary-General on Women, Peace, and Security," September 2015; "Report of the Secretary-General on Women and Peace and Security," September 2014, p. 27; Coomaraswamy et al.

47. Paffenholz et al., 2016; Coomaraswamy et al.; Chang et al.

48. DCAF, "Gender-Sensitive Disarmament, Demobilisation and Reintegration," 2009; DCAF, "Gender and Security Sector Reform: Examples from the Ground," 2011, pp. 21–23.

49. Interviews conducted by Dyan Mazurana and Khristopher Carlson, "From Combat to Community: Women and Girls of Sierra Leone," Hunt Alternatives, 2004, http:// peacewomen.org/assets/file/Resources/NGO/PartPPGIssueDisp_CombatTo Communty_WomenWagePeace_2004.pdf.

50. Raghabendra Chattopadhyay and Esther Duflo, "Women as Policy Makers: Evidence from a Randomized Policy Experiment in India," *Econometrica* 72, no. 5, September 2004, pp. 1409–1443; see also Lori Beaman et al, "Women Politicians, Gender Bias, and Policy-Making in Rural India," UNICEF, December 2006.

51. UN Women, "The Effect of Gender Equality Programming on Humanitarian Outcomes," United Nations Entity for Gender Equality and the Empowerment of Women, 2015.

52. Jacqueline H.R. DeMeritt et al., "Female Participation and Civil War Relapse," *Civil Wars* 16, no. 3, 2014, p. 362; O'Reilly, "Inclusive Security and Peaceful Societies."

53. Melander, "Gender Equality and Intrastate Armed Conflict;" Erik Melander, "Political Gender Equality and State Human Rights Abuse," *Journal of Peace Research* 42, no. 2, March 2005, pp. 149–166.

54. Ricardo Hausmann et al., "The Global Gender Gap Report 2010," World Economic Forum, 2010; Patricia Justino et al., "Quantifying the Impact of Women's Participation

in Post-Conflict Economic Recovery," Households in Conflict Network Working Paper 131, University of Sussex Institute of Development Studies, November 2012, pp. 20–23; Patti Petesch, "Women's Empowerment Arising From Violent Conflict and Recovery: Life Stories From Four Middle-Income Countries," USAID, May 20, 2011.

55. Alice Nderitu and Jacqueline O'Neill, "Getting to the Point of Inclusion: Seven Myths Standing in the Way of Women Waging Peace," Institute for Inclusive Security, June 2013, http://inclusivesecurity.org/wp-content/uploads/2014/02/Getting-to-the-Point-of-Inclusion.pdf.

56. Chang et al.; O'Reilly, "Inclusive Security and Peaceful Societies;" Paffenholz et al., 2016.

57. McKinsey Global Institute, "The Power of Parity: How Advancing Women's Equality Can Add $12 Trillion to Global Growth," September 2015; World Economic Forum, "Global Gender Gap Report 2015," November 19, 2015.

58. O'Reilly et al., "Reimagining Peacemaking."

59. Erin Marie Saltman and Ross Frenett, "Female Radicalization to ISIS and the Role of CVE: Motivations, Experiences and Engagement," in *A Man's World? Exploring the Roles of Women in Counter Terrorism and Violent Extremism*, eds. Naureen Chowdhury Fink, Sara Zeiger, and Rafia Bhulai, Hedayah, Global Center on Cooperative Security, 2016, p. 142.

60. Enrique Alvarez and Tania Palencia Prado, "Guatemala's Peace Process: Context, Analysis, and Evaluation," *Conciliation Resources*, no. 13, 2002.

61. Walda Barrios Klee, quoted in "Women Leading Peace," p. 62; María Marroquín, quoted in "Women Leading Peace," p. 65.

62. Chang et al.; Sanam Naraghi Anderlini, "Women, Peace and Security: A Policy Audit," International Alert, June 2001, pp. 23–24.

63. Kate Fearon, "Northern Ireland's Women's Coalition: Institutionalising a Political Voice and Ensuring Representation," Conciliation Resources, 2002, http://c-r.org/accord/public-participation/northern-ireland-s-women-s-coalition-institutionalising-political-voice.

64. Chang et al.; Naraghi Anderlini, *Women Building Peace.*

65. Chang et al.

66. Dorina Bekoe and Christina Parajon, "Women's Role in Liberia's Reconstruction," United States Institute of Peace, May 1, 2007, http://usip.org/publications/women-s-role-in-liberia-s-reconstruction.

67. "Leymah Gbowee in Her Own Words," PBS, September 13, 2011, http://pbs.org/wnet/women-war-and-peace/features/the-president-will-see-you-now.

68. DCAF, "The Liberian National Police's Female Recruitment Programme," 2009, pp. 66–67.

69. Jasmin Nario-Galace and Frances Piscano, "Philippines: Security Council Resolution 1325; Civil Society Monitoring Report 2011," Global Network of Women Peacebuilders, 2011.

70. Yasmin Busran-Lao, "Philippines: Women and Inclusivity in the Mindanao Peace Process," Conciliation Resources, 2014, http://c-r.org/accord/legitimacy-and-peace-processes/philippines-women-and-inclusivity-mindanao-peace-process.

71. Mary Ann M. Arnado, "Women's Involvement in Conflict Early Warning Systems: Moving From Rhetoric to Reality in Mindanao," Centre for Humanitarian Dialogue, October 2012, http://www.hdcentre.org/uploads/tx_news/77WomensinvolvementinconflictearlywarningsystemsFINAL_2.pdf.

72. "G7 Foreign Ministers' Meeting," Ministry of Foreign Affairs Japan, Hiroshima, Japan, April 10–11, 2016, http://mofa.go.jp/files/000147440.pdf; "Women, Peace and Security," North Atlantic Treaty Organization, October 29, 2015, http://nato.int/NATO1325.

73. Paffenholz et al., 2016.

74. "DOD Is Expanding Combat Service Opportunities for Women, but Should Monitor Long-Term Integration Progress," United States Government Accountability Office, GAO-15-589, July 2015.

75. Kristy N. Kamarck, "Diversity, Inclusion, and Equal Opportunity in the Armed Services: Background and Issues for Congress," Congressional Research Service, December 23, 2016, http://fas.org/sgp/crs/natsec/R44321.pdf.

76. "Total Workforce: Distribution by Race/Ethnicity and Sex," USAID, last updated September 30, 2015, http://usaid.gov/sites/default/files/documents/1874/USAID%20 U.S%20Direct%20Hire%20Workforce%20Demographics%20as%20of%20FY% 202015.pdf; "What Role Do Women Play in the Department of State," *Discover Diplomacy*, U.S. Department of State, http://diplomacy.state.gov/discoverdiplomacy/ diplomacy101/people/205643.htm.

77. Rosabeth Moss Kanter, *Men and Women of the Corporation* (New York: Basic Books, 1997), pp. 381–395.

78. Paffenholz et al., 2016.

79. "Report of the Secretary-General on Women's Participation in Peacebuilding (A/65/354-S/2010/466)," United Nations, 2010, pp. 1–2; "UN Strategic Results Framework on Women, Peace and Security: 2011–2020," United Nations, July 2011.

80. "Report of the Secretary-General on Women's Participation in Peacebuilding (A/65/354-S/2010/466)," pp. 1–2; "UN Strategic Results Framework on Women, Peace and Security: 2011–2020."

About the Authors

Jamille Bigio is an adjunct senior fellow in the Women and Foreign Policy program at the Council on Foreign Relations. In the Obama administration, Bigio served as director for human rights and gender on the White House National Security Council. From 2009 to 2013, she served as senior advisor to U.S. ambassador-at-large for global women's issues, Melanne Verveer, at the Department of State. In addition, Bigio was detailed to the office of the undersecretary of defense for policy and to the U.S. Mission to the African Union. She led the interagency launch of the U.S. National Action Plan on Women, Peace, and Security, an effort for which she was recognized with the U.S. Department of State Superior Honor Award and the U.S. Department of Defense Secretary of Defense Honor Award. Previously, at the United Nations, she worked to strengthen disaster management in Africa and the Middle East. Bigio has worked at the grassroots level for public health nongovernmental organizations, and her research on development, human rights, and displacement was supported by the World Bank and the Brookings Institution. She graduated Phi Beta Kappa from the University of Maryland and received her master's degree from the Harvard Kennedy School.

Rachel Vogelstein is a senior fellow and director of the Women and Foreign Policy Program at the Council on Foreign Relations. She is also an adjunct professor of gender and U.S. foreign policy at Georgetown University Law Center. From 2009 to 2012, Vogelstein was director of policy and senior advisor in the Office of Global Women's Issues within the Office of the Secretary of State at the U.S. Department of State, and served as a member of the White House Council on Women and Girls. Following her tenure at the State Department, Vogelstein served as the director of women and girls programs in the Office of Hillary Clinton at the Clinton Foundation, where she oversaw the development of the No

Ceilings initiative and provided guidance on domestic and global women's issues. Prior to joining the State Department, Vogelstein was an advisor to Hillary Clinton, serving as an advisor to Clinton's first U.S. Senate campaign and as assistant counsel to Clinton's 2008 presidential campaign. Vogelstein also was senior counsel at the National Women's Law Center in Washington, DC, where she specialized in women's health and reproductive rights. She graduated magna cum laude from Columbia University's Barnard College and cum laude from Georgetown University Law Center, where she was executive editor of the *Georgetown Law Journal.*

Advisory Committee for *How Women's Participation in Conflict Prevention and Resolution Advances U.S. Interests*

John Allen
U.S. Marine Corps (Ret.);
Brookings Institution

Christine Chinkin
London School of Economics
and Political Science

Michèle Flournoy
Center for a New American Security

Anne Marie Goetz
New York University

Rangina Hamidi
Kandahar Treasure

Swanee Hunt
Inclusive Security

Saroj Kumar Jha
World Bank Group

Dan Leaf
U.S. Air Force (Ret.);
Asia-Pacific Center for Security Studies

William K. Lietzau
PAE; Former Marine Corps Judge Advocate

David Morrison
Australian Army (Ret.)

Alaa Murabit
The Voice of Libyan Women

Thania Paffenholz
Graduate Institute, Inclusive Peace
and Transition Initiative

Anders Fogh Rasmussen
Rasmussen Global; Former Prime Minister
of Denmark and Secretary-General of NATO

Sarah Sewall
U.S. Department of State, Peacekeeping
and Humanitarian Assistance

Paul B. Stares
Council on Foreign Relations

Don Steinberg
World Learning

Suzy Vares-Lum
U.S. Pacific Command

Melanne Verveer
Georgetown Institute for Women, Peace,
and Security

www.ingramcontent.com/pod-product-compliance
Lightning Source LLC
Chambersburg PA
CBHW051431270326
41933CB00022B/3487